LION LIGHTS

my invention that made peace with lions

by Richard Turere
with Shelly Pollock

illustrated by
Sonia Possentini

TILBURY HOUSE PUBLISHERS

DEDICATIONS

As the saying goes, "It takes a village to raise a child."
I would like to dedicate this book to everyone who has greatly
supported me to become who I am now. Blessings upon you!!
—Richard

To my husband, Kim, for being a constant inspiration and my rock
of support, and to all children who want to do amazing things.
—Shelly

To children and their discoveries everywhere.
—Sonia

What is that sound?

Is it the wind rustling
the tall grass, or is it
what I fear most?

Lions!

Lions lurking . . .

... waiting to leap and kill my father's cows.

The cows are my family's meat, milk, and hides. They are our family's wealth, and my job is to protect them. I must not fail.

I am nine years old.

That nine-year-old boy
was me, not so long ago.
Now I, Richard Turere, am
older, but I remember how
scared I was back then.

My family's farm borders the south
side of Nairobi National Park in
Kenya, where wild animals roam,
and those animals include the king
of them all. Lions!

Lions need food, and a cow is much
easier to grab than a zippy zebra.

My family are Maasai. Once our people roamed Kenya's plains with our cows and goats, moving with the dry and wet seasons to find good grass. Now we live in small villages called *manyattas*, but we still have to protect our herds from lions.

When I was six, I began tending our sheep and goats. Three years later my father chose me to herd the cattle. It was a great honor.

In the dry season our animals needed to graze far from the farm to find pasture and water, and I had to herd them home again each night. I missed a lot of school, and when I did go to classes, it was hard to stay awake.

I watched planes flying overhead and dreamed of being a in a plane myself, exploring the world.

Each night I herded our cows into their boma. Its fence of thorny acacia branches kept the cattle inside but couldn't keep lions out, no matter how tall and sturdy we tried to build it. The lions couldn't see the cows, but they could smell them!

Like other Maasai herders, I tried many ploys to keep lions away.

I built fires fueled by cow dung outside the boma, but lions walked around or between the flames.

I made a scarecrow. It worked the first night, but lions are smart. They weren't fooled for long by my simple trick.

Long ago, a Maasai boy had to kill a lion
with a spear in order to become a warrior.

That time passed but was not forgotten. Desperate Maasai farmers still speared lions or even poisoned them.

Tourists come from all over the world to see Kenya's wild animals. That would end if the lions disappeared.

Wildlife conservationists tried to find an answer. The government tried paying farmers for dead cows, but the payments were too small. They tried building chain link fences and providing guard dogs, but that was too expensive.

Lions kept killing cows, and Maasai herders kept killing lions.

I was always curious. While other boys played warriors and lions, I tinkered with electronic gadgets. Without books or anyone to help me, I had to teach myself. To learn, I took everything apart.

Once I broke open my family's TV to see if the people inside were real.

My mother was even more upset the day I took her new radio apart—but I learned a lot about electronics!

When I was eleven years old, a morning came when I started hating lions. I found my father's only bull dead inside the boma.

That meant we'd have to buy another bull or borrow one from another farm to get new calves. It was like waking up in the morning to find you have lost everything. All your savings are gone.

I knew then that I had to outsmart
the lions or end up hating them.
But how? No one in Africa had
found a solution. How could I?

When I walked around the boma with a flashlight, I noticed that
the lions stayed away. They were afraid of my moving light. But
I couldn't guard the cows every night. I needed to be sleeping
in my bed! If only my flashlight could move by itself.

Then I had an idea.

I knew something about how electronics
worked. Maybe I could use my knowledge to
trick those prowlers.

I gathered parts. I came upon a smashed-up flashlight with a light bulb. I found a discarded turn-signal flasher from a small motorcycle.

I found a switch. I borrowed bits of wire. My father gave me an old car battery that I had to carry to and from town to charge every two days, a three-kilometer hike each way.

I tried many experiments. I gave myself and my little brother electrical shocks. My parents built a small shed to get my constant tinkering out of the house. They didn't think my ideas could work. Neither did our neighbors. But each failure gave me a chance to ask why and try again.

Finally, when I was twelve, I was ready to put everything together. I wound bits of wire around the boma's fenceposts, then twisted flashlight bulbs into the circuit. I aimed the bulbs outward, where lions lurked. I connected the bulbs to a switch.

As night fell, I flipped the switch, my heart beating fast.

First one small bulb flashed. Then the next one. Then the next.

One by one, all around the boma, lights flashed.

And the lions stayed away. They must have thought my whole family was walking around!

But would they catch on to this
trick like they had the scarecrow?
The next night I waited and
watched again: The lights blinked
on and off, on and off. And all
night long, the lions stayed away.

MY LIGHTS WORKED!
They worked the next night and the night after that, too.
I slept well!

I called my invention Lion Lights.

Word spread quickly. Soon my neighbors wanted Lion Lights too.

I did not realize the importance of my little invention, or how my life was about to change. One day, some important people came to see me. They, too, were amazed by what I had done. They said no one had ever thought of this.

My homemade Lion Lights had cost less than ten dollars to make. They were simple, quick to install, and movable.

I had saved our family's cows, which is a Maasai warrior's duty.

Now my lights are being used around the world, and best of all, I finally outsmarted the lions!

About the Maasai

A Maasai legend says that one god, Enkai, created the world with three groups of people. The first group, the Torrobo, were hunters and depended on wild animals and honey. The second group, the Kikuyus, were farmers. The third group were the Maasai, and Enkai entrusted the cattle of the world to them. Cows are central to the Maasai people's identity.

According to oral history, the Maasai ancestors came from North Africa. They migrated south along the Nile Valley about three hundred years ago, settling along the borders of Kenya and Tanzania to graze their cattle. They brought with them their language, Maa; in fact, the word Maasai itself means "people who speak Maa." It is an oral language—not written—with a strong storytelling tradition. Today the Maasai people also speak Swahili and English.

The Maasai territory reached its greatest extent in the 1800s, occupying the vast arid grasslands of the Great Rift Valley where many national parks and game reserves are located today. For hundreds of years, the Maasai lived in their traditional way, following the seasons in search of grass and water for their herds. It remains true to this day that the more cattle a family owns, the richer that family is. So important are cows and goats to a Maasai herder that he does not even need to count them; he knows each one by sight.

The Maasai were the dominant people of Kenya in the late 1800s, but they struggled to preserve their territory when European settlers arrived. Their spears were no match for armed British troops, and their lawyers never stood a fair chance in British courtrooms. In 1904, the Maasai signed an agreement in which they lost much of their best land, and a second agreement in 1911 transferred their best remaining northern land (Laikipia) to white settlers. Together, the two treaties ceded about two-thirds of the Maasai's ancestral lands to the colonial government, and the people were resettled in less fertile parts of Kenya and Tanzania.

Today about one million Maasai people live in Kenya, and a greater number live in Tanzania. They are one of the best-known African tribes, famous for their colorful culture, customs, and traditional dress. Their villages, or *manyattas*, are close to national parks and game reserves, making the Maasai territories one of Africa's leading tourist destinations.

A traditional Maasai *enkaji*, or hut, is loaf-shaped and small, with only one or two rooms.

The ceilings are low, making it hard for these tall people to stand up. The framework is formed with timber poles fixed in the ground, and a lattice of smaller branches is interwoven around the poles. Then a mixture of cow dung and urine is applied, which becomes as strong as cement when it dries, making the hut waterproof. Sticks and grass are plastered around this framework. Nowadays, however, tin roofs and other modern materials are transforming these dwellings.

In the 1960s, the Maasai started replacing their traditional clothing of animal skins with cotton cloth. Women and men prefer a bright red cloth called a *shuka*, which is worn around their shoulders as a cape or around their waist as a skirt. Bright red is a proud signifier of Maasai culture and identity. Maasai sandals, until recently made from cowhide, are now more commonly made of tire strips or plastic.

The Maasai face severe challenges in the twenty-first century. Droughts are more severe because of climate change. Cattle diseases are prevalent, and Maasai herders are being squeezed into smaller and smaller areas. As their grazing land has shrunk, so have their herds. And they must try to protect their cows from the lions that prowl the night from the nearby wildlife reserves.

Maasai farmers tried many ways to keep their cows safe. As Richard tells in the story, nothing worked—not fences, dogs, scarecrows, thorn-tree barriers, or fixed lights. In desperation, some Maasai farmers shot or poisoned lions, but this could not continue because lions are a threatened and protected species and are key to Kenya's tourism. Richard's simple and elegant invention, Lion Lights, solved a problem that had defeated the experts. Scientists and conservationists across Africa testify to the importance of his $10 solution.

Many Maasai have moved from the countryside to Nairobi, the capital of Kenya, and to other cities looking for jobs. Those who have remained on their farms—like Richard's family—augment their income with gardens of maize, beans, rice, and other crops. Many Maasai have become entrepreneurs, guiding safaris or selling beads, masks, and wood carvings to tourists. Some Maasai villages invite visitors to experience their traditions and culture for a fee.

Yet, despite all these changes, urban Maasai people return home whenever possible to wear their *shuka* and sandals and honor their proud, beautiful, ageless traditions.

Maasai Words

acacia tree [ah-KAY-sha]: A common thorny tree of the African veld and savanna.

asante: Swahili for "Thank you."

ashe oleng: Maa for "Thank you very much."

boma: An enclosure for livestock that is surrounded by a circular fence of thorny branches.

Enkai: The Maasai god who created the world.

enkaji [en-KAH-jee]: A traditional Maasai hut built (usually by women) from mud, cow dung, and wood.

enkang [EN-kahng]: A group of huts arranged in a circle, built by men and fenced in with thorned acacia branches.

habari: Swahili for "How are you?"

inkajijik: A group of houses (enkaji).

jambo: Swahili for "Hello."

Maa [mah]: The official language of the Maasai.

Maasai [MAH-sigh or mah-SIGH]: A semi-nomadic Native African people.

Maasai Mara: The Maasai homeland in Kenya, which stretches across the Serengeti Plain into Tanzania.

manyatta: A small village comprised of huts arranged in a circle.

orinka: A club to throw or hit with.

Serengeti Plain: The name for the vast grasslands of Maasailand, covering parts of Kenya and Tanzania. This vital ecosystem hosts the largest population of lions in the world.

shuka: A bright red cape.

sopa: The Maa word for "Hello/Hi."

Learning More

Chamberlin, Mary and Rich. *Mama Panya's Pancakes*. Barefoot Books, 2005.

Deedy, Carma Agra. *14 Cows for America*. Peachtree, 2009.

Fifth Graders P.S. 107. *One Special Lion: The Story of Sion*. Independently published, 2020.

Kamkwamba, William, and Bryan Mealer. *The Boy Who Harnessed the Wind*. Dial, 2012.

Kreb, Laurie. *We All Went on Safari*. Barefoot Books, 2004.

McBrier, Page. *Beatrice's Goat*. Aladdin, 2004.

Miranda, Paul. *One Plastic Bag*. Millbrook, 2015.

Smith Millway, Katie. *One Hen: How One Small Loan Made a Big Difference*. Kids Can Press, 2008.

Verde, Susan. *The Water Princess*. G.P. Putman, 2016.

Winter, Jeanette. *Wangari's Trees of Peace: A True Story from Africa*. Harcourt, 2008.

Online Resources

"Maasai," http://encyclopedia.kids.net.au/page/ma/Maasai

"Maasai," www.everyculture.com/wc/Tajikistan-to-Zimbabwe/Maasai.html

"Maasai People, Kenya," www.maasai-association.org/maasai.html

"Maasai Wilderness Conservation Trust," http://maasaiwilderness.org/maasai

"The Maasai," www.sheppardsoftware.com/Africaweb/factfile/africauniquefact18.htm

"The Maasai Tribe," www.arcgis.com/apps/MapJournal/index.html?appid=9c4dc3494fc8 4abaa95d380abdf55409

Tilbury House Publishers
Thomaston, Maine
www.tilburyhouse.com

Designed by Frame25 Productions
Printed in South Korea

Richard Turere is an undergraduate student at the African Leadership University, where he is studying Global Challenges with a focus on wildlife conservation. Richard shared his Lion Lights with the world at the TED Global Stage in California. He received a special commendation from Africa Leadership Awards for his critical role in protecting and creating awareness around the crisis facing lions in Kenya. He is recognized as Kenya's youngest patent inventor and, in 2018, received the Anzisha prize award. In 2020 he became a National Geographic Young Explorer, and he was a finalist in the Future for Nature awards in 2021. Visit Richard at www.lion-lights.org.

Shelly Pollock taught remedial reading and math to children and adults in the US for twenty-five years. She hopes that *Lion Lights*, her debut picture book, will inspire children everywhere to realize that no matter how young they may be or how big their challenges, they can accomplish anything. Visit Shelly at www.ShellyPollock.com.

Sonia Maria Luce Possentini is an award-winning illustrator in Modena, Italy, and a professor of illustration at the International School of Comics in Reggio Emilia. She has illustrated thirteen children's books, including *Night Creatures* (2021) and *Hold on to Your Music* (2021).